MEDAVI

Prompt Engineering for UX

Contents

1

Introduction

L et's start by imagining a world where every designer, regardless of experience, can bring innovative ideas to life instantly, at the click of a button. What if, instead of spending hours or days meticulously sketching out a wireframe or iterating on design elements, you could describe your vision in a simple sentence and have AI deliver options in seconds? That future isn't far away; in fact, it's already here, and Generative AI is making it happen.

The Evolving Role of AI in Design

In the past, design was a craft entirely dependent on human effort. The creativity, intuition, and problem-solving skills of a designer couldn't be easily automated or outsourced to machines. Designers spent years honing their skills, learning to interpret user needs, and translating abstract ideas into tangible products. But with the advent of Generative AI, things are changing rapidly.

Artificial Intelligence (AI) is no longer confined to the realm of data crunching or automating simple tasks. It has evolved to become a collaborator, capable of augmenting human creativity. In the world of User Experience (UX) design, this means AI can now assist in everything from wireframing and prototyping to creating visual elements and even running usability tests. AI is essentially becoming an integral part of the design toolkit.

But make no mistake: AI is not here to replace designers. Rather, it's here to help them work faster, smarter, and more creatively. The future of design will be about how well you collaborate with AI to bring your visions to life. And to make this collaboration work, UX designers will need to learn a new skill: **prompt engineering**.

Why UX Designers Need to Embrace Prompt Engineering

If you're wondering what prompt engineering is, think of it as the art of communicating with AI. Just as designers have learned to master design tools like Photoshop or Sketch, the next wave of essential skills involves writing prompts that guide AI to deliver the design outputs you need.

Here's the thing about AI: it's powerful, but it doesn't think like a human. It requires clear instructions to give you exactly what you want. Imagine asking an AI to design a login screen. If your prompt is too vague—"Create a login screen"—you'll get something generic. But if your prompt is specific—"Create a login screen for a travel app with a minimalist design, using pastel colors, and incorporating a fingerprint authentication feature"—AI will deliver something much closer to what you need.

2

Learning how to craft these prompts effectively is what will set the best designers apart. By understanding the nuances of prompt engineering, UX designers can shape AI's output to align with their vision. This isn't just about saving time; it's about unlocking creative potential that wasn't previously accessible. AI can generate multiple variations, explore design options you may not have thought of, and even propose innovative solutions to complex problems.

In these competitive markets, where the demand for high-quality, user-centric products is ever-growing, AI can help you stay ahead of the curve. Whether you're working for a tech startup in Silicon Valley or a design agency in Toronto, mastering AI through prompt engineering could give you a significant edge.

Overview of How Generative AI Can Revolutionize the Design Process

Generative AI is like having an ever-ready design partner. Traditionally, UX designers followed a linear process: you start with research, create wireframes, get feedback, iterate, and then move to high-fidelity designs. Each step requires time, effort, and constant back-and-forth with stakeholders or developers.

Generative AI changes this by drastically speeding up the iterative cycles. Here's how:

1. **Rapid Prototyping**: With the right prompts, AI can generate multiple design prototypes in a fraction of the time. You can input high-level concepts and get back layouts,

user flows, or entire screen designs that are ready to be tested or refined.

2. **Design Exploration**: One of the biggest advantages of AI is that it can think outside the box—literally. It can generate dozens of creative solutions to a single design problem. You no longer need to worry about getting stuck in one design direction; AI provides new perspectives and possibilities you may not have considered.

3. **Efficiency in Design Systems**: AI can help you create and manage design systems more effectively. It can instantly generate components that are consistent with your brand's guidelines, making it easier to scale designs across projects. Imagine not having to manually recreate every button, icon, or layout—AI can do it for you in seconds, ensuring consistency across your designs.

4. **User Testing & Feedback**: AI can also assist in the user testing phase. By analyzing user interactions and generating insights, AI helps designers quickly identify areas for improvement. This reduces the guesswork and makes the iteration process more data-driven.

5. **Personalization at Scale**: In the era of personalized user experiences, AI enables designers to create dynamic, customizable interfaces that adapt to individual user needs. AI can generate multiple versions of a design, allowing you to cater to diverse user segments without the need for manual customization.

In short, Generative AI not only saves time but also expands the scope of what's possible. It amplifies creativity by automating repetitive tasks and freeing designers to focus on solving complex problems and crafting truly user-centered experiences.

For UX designers, this means you can now bring more ideas to the table, test them quickly, and refine them faster. It's a tool that transforms the way we think about design, moving us from linear, time-consuming processes to dynamic, agile workflows. In the future, UX design won't just be about what you can create—it'll be about what you can co-create with AI. And prompt engineering is the key to unlocking that future.

* * *

These foundational tools help UX designers understand AI's role and potential in design:

1. **ChatGPT** – For exploring AI-driven ideation and design brainstorming.
2. **DeepL** – To enhance content localization and translations in UX for global reach.
3. **Notion AI** – For organizing and generating content related to UX design processes.
4. **Figma** – Equipped with AI plugins to assist with collaborative design work.
5. **Copy.ai** – Generates copy for UX/UI text, making it ideal for brainstorming.
6. **Lucidchart** – Assists with flowchart and wireframe creation.
7. **Grammarly** – To check the readability of UX text elements.
8. **Otter.ai** – For AI transcription, useful in user interviews and research.
9. **QuillBot** – Paraphrasing tool to reword and refine content.
10. **Runway ML** – Focused on video editing and other creative assets for UX.

2

Understanding Generative AI in UX Design

The concept of Generative AI might sound a bit technical at first, but once you grasp it, you'll see how powerful it is for UX design. We're talking about a tool that can assist you in creating, iterating, and refining designs, all at an accelerated pace. It's like having a highly skilled design assistant who's ready to respond to your every idea, suggestion, or challenge, 24/7. But to fully take advantage of this potential, it's crucial to understand what Generative AI is, how it works, and why it's so relevant to modern UX and product design.

What is Generative AI?

Generative AI refers to a class of artificial intelligence systems designed to generate content, whether it be text, images, designs, or even entire products. Unlike traditional AI, which follows pre-programmed rules and logic to perform specific tasks, Generative AI models are trained on massive datasets, learning patterns and generating outputs based on user inputs.

In simple terms, you give AI a prompt—say, "design a landing page for a fitness app"—and the AI uses its understanding of the task to generate a design for you.

For UX designers, this means AI can handle a significant amount of the groundwork. Instead of laboring over endless revisions or starting from scratch with every new idea, Generative AI can provide a foundation, a starting point that you can build on, tweak, and perfect. It's a massive shift in how design work gets done, from creation to iteration.

To put it into perspective: think of Generative AI as an intelligent design collaborator. It's not taking over your job, but rather, it's accelerating the process and giving you more time to focus on strategic and creative thinking. And in an industry that's increasingly fast-paced and competitive, this efficiency is invaluable.

* * *

How AI Models Work: An Overview of GPT and Other AI Tools

At the heart of Generative AI are models like GPT (Generative Pre-trained Transformer), developed by OpenAI. Models like GPT are trained on vast amounts of data, from websites and books to product designs and user flows. This training allows them to learn patterns, understand context, and generate new content based on the input they receive.

Let's break it down:

- **Training Phase**: The AI model is fed massive datasets, which it uses to learn the relationships between words, phrases, and even entire paragraphs. In the case of visual models like DALL·E, it learns the relationships between pixels, colors, shapes, and design elements.
- **Generating Outputs**: Once trained, the AI can take a prompt—like "create a minimalist user interface for a weather app"—and generate a new design based on the patterns it has learned. The model uses probabilities to determine which design elements, colors, and layouts best fit the given prompt.
- **Refinement & Iteration**: What makes these AI models even more useful is their ability to refine outputs based on feedback. For example, if you don't like the design generated by the AI, you can modify your prompt or give additional instructions. This back-and-forth creates a dynamic interaction, where the AI becomes a design partner that learns from your input.

Key models you might encounter in Generative AI include:

- **GPT (Generative Pre-trained Transformer)**: Primarily used for text generation, but also useful in UX for generating user personas, content ideas, and even descriptions of UI components.
- **DALL·E**: An AI tool designed for generating images from text prompts. This is incredibly useful for UX designers when creating visual elements or getting design inspiration.
- **MidJourney**: A newer AI tool that excels in generating artistic and design-oriented visuals based on text inputs, helping UX designers quickly visualize concepts.

- **Stable Diffusion**: Another image-generation AI that can create complex visuals from prompts, useful for generating product images, logos, or UI components.

These tools operate on a basic principle: the better the input (your prompt), the better the output (the design). This is why prompt engineering becomes such a critical skill. Learning to frame your design requests in a way that AI understands can make the difference between getting a vague result and a highly refined, creative design.

* * *

The Relevance of AI in UX and Product Design

So why should UX designers care about AI? The relevance of AI in UX design boils down to one word: **scalability**.

In a world where user experience is central to product success, scaling designs efficiently is key. Think of the countless hours spent on tweaking button sizes, aligning components, or testing different layouts. Now, imagine if AI could handle these tasks for you. This is not about cutting corners—it's about making the design process more agile, freeing up your mental bandwidth to focus on higher-level, strategic challenges.

Here are a few ways AI is particularly relevant to UX and product design:

1. **Speeding Up Prototyping and Iteration**: One of the most

time-consuming aspects of UX design is the iteration process. You create a prototype, get feedback, make changes, and repeat. Generative AI can accelerate this by instantly generating new design options based on user feedback. Designers can then focus on refining the best options rather than starting from scratch each time.

2. **Personalization at Scale**: In today's market, users expect personalized experiences. AI can help generate custom interfaces or user flows based on different personas or user data. This makes it easier for designers to create personalized products without manually designing different versions for each user segment.

3. **Enhancing Creativity**: While AI might not replace a designer's creative intuition, it can certainly enhance it. By generating design variations, AI can push boundaries, offering ideas and solutions a designer may not have thought of. This leads to more innovative product designs that stand out in crowded markets like those in North America.

4. **Automating Repetitive Tasks**: Many UX tasks—like aligning components, adjusting color schemes, or creating icons—are repetitive. AI can automate these tasks, allowing designers to spend more time on user research, strategy, and crafting delightful user experiences. Essentially, AI takes care of the mundane, giving designers more room to be creative.

5. **Data-Driven Design Decisions**: AI doesn't just generate designs; it can also analyze user data and suggest improvements. For example, it can recommend tweaks to a design based on user behavior patterns or usability testing data. This makes the design process more data-driven and

user-centric, ensuring that final products meet user needs effectively.

* * *

Top AI tools that help UX designers understand AI models, their architecture, and integration:

1. OpenAI API (GPT-4) - Comprehensive text-based model for exploring AI interaction.
2. Midjourney - For AI-powered image generation, ideal for visual inspiration.
3. DALL·E - Generates custom visuals from text prompts.
4. Stable Diffusion - Open-source AI model for generating complex designs.
5. AI Dungeon - Useful for creative ideation and story-driven UX scenarios.
6. Hugging Face - Hosts numerous AI models, enabling experimentation.
7. Craiyon - Formerly DALL·E Mini, a free option for image generation.
8. Deep Dream Generator - Generates unique visuals using neural networks.
9. ChatGPT Plugins - Expands OpenAI's capabilities with plugins that can aid in UX.
10. Rasa - For creating conversational AI, useful in chatbots and user experience.

3

The Basics of Prompt Engineering

S o, you've heard that Generative AI can be a game-changer for UX design. But how do you get AI to understand what you want? How do you make sure it generates design solutions that actually meet your needs? That's where **prompt engineering** comes into play.

Prompt engineering is the skill of crafting instructions for AI in a way that leads to the best possible outcome. It's not about giving the AI a simple command and hoping for the best—it's about being strategic, clear, and detailed. Just like in UX design, where the details of user flows, wireframes, and feedback loops can make or break a product, the details in your AI prompts will determine how effective and creative your AI-generated designs are.

What is Prompt Engineering?

Let's start with a simple definition: **Prompt engineering is the process of designing and refining the input (or "prompt") you**

give to AI to guide it toward producing the desired output. In the context of UX design, this could mean giving AI a prompt to generate a wireframe for a mobile app, design a set of icons, or even suggest a new user flow.

Think of it like communicating with another human being, but instead of speaking in natural language, you're giving AI specific, structured instructions. The clearer and more precise your instructions, the more useful and relevant the AI's output will be.

For example, if you tell AI to "create a login screen," you might get something generic and not very useful. But if you tell AI to "create a minimalist login screen for a fitness app, with pastel colors, a logo on top, and options for fingerprint and face recognition," you're giving it enough detail to generate something much closer to what you actually need.

In short, prompt engineering is all about maximizing the potential of AI by giving it the right information to work with.

* * *

The Anatomy of a Great Prompt

Not all prompts are created equal. A well-crafted prompt is like a good design brief—it provides the AI with all the context, constraints, and goals needed to generate an output that's not just functional, but creative and aligned with your vision. Let's break down the elements that make up a great prompt.

1. **Clarity**: Your prompt needs to be clear and unambiguous. The AI doesn't understand nuance in the same way a human does, so being vague will result in generic or irrelevant outputs. Instead of saying "design a home page," be specific: "Design a home page for a food delivery service that highlights user testimonials, includes a search bar, and has call-to-action buttons for signing up."

2. **Context**: AI responds best when it has context. Provide as much relevant background information as possible. For example, "Design a landing page for an eco-friendly product company targeting young adults aged 18-30, focusing on sustainability and minimalism." This tells the AI who the target audience is and what themes or values the design should reflect.

3. **Constraints**: Every design has limitations, whether it's color schemes, layout styles, or functionality. Including constraints in your prompt helps the AI avoid designs that don't fit your project. For instance, you could specify, "Use a two-column layout and stick to a blue and white color palette."

4. **Tone and Style**: Just like UX design has certain aesthetics or visual styles, AI-generated designs can be guided by the tone you want to set. For example, you might ask for a "playful and colorful dashboard for a kids' educational app" or a "clean, professional UI for a corporate finance platform."

5. **Actionable Details**: The more actionable details you provide, the more refined the AI's output will be. Instead of saying "design an app," you could say, "Design a mobile app for a ride-sharing service, with an emphasis on simplicity, showing user locations on a map, and including

buttons for requesting a ride and paying via credit card."

Here's a quick formula for structuring an effective prompt: **[Action] + [Design Context] + [Target Audience] + [Style/Constraints] + [Specific Details]**

Example: "Create a high-fidelity wireframe for a health tracking app designed for people aged 40+, with a focus on simplicity and ease of use. The screen should include a dashboard showing step count, heart rate, and calorie intake, using a dark mode color scheme."

* * *

Why Prompt Structure Matters in AI-Generated Design Solutions

The structure of your prompt is essential because it directly impacts the AI's ability to generate high-quality, relevant design solutions. Let's think of prompt structure as the difference between a well-organized design process and one that's chaotic. If your instructions are scattered and incomplete, the AI won't be able to produce useful results. A clear, well-structured prompt serves as a roadmap for the AI.

Here's why prompt structure matters:

1. **Avoids Ambiguity**: A structured prompt leaves less room for misunderstanding. AI doesn't "guess" in the same way humans do—it follows the instructions exactly as given. If the prompt is vague or lacks structure, the AI might

produce outputs that miss the mark entirely. By clearly stating the action, context, and constraints, you minimize the chances of receiving irrelevant designs.

2. **Speeds Up Iteration**: With a well-structured prompt, the AI can deliver outputs that are closer to what you need from the get-go. This reduces the time spent on back-and-forth iterations and helps you reach a refined design faster. In a fast-paced design environment, especially in competitive markets like the US and Canada, this speed can be a huge advantage.

3. **Enhances Creativity**: A well-structured prompt doesn't limit creativity—it enhances it. By providing the right amount of detail and direction, you allow the AI to explore creative solutions within a specific framework. Think of it like giving a painter a canvas, brushes, and a theme—the structure guides creativity without stifling it.

4. **Aligns with Project Goals**: Design is always tied to project goals, whether it's improving user experience, increasing engagement, or driving conversions. A structured prompt ensures that the AI-generated designs are aligned with these goals. For instance, if the goal is to create a highly engaging onboarding flow, your prompt should reflect that by specifying interactive elements and user-friendly navigation.

* * *

Common Pitfalls to Avoid in Prompt Writing

16

While writing prompts for AI might seem straightforward, there are some common mistakes that can lead to less-than-ideal results. Here are a few pitfalls to avoid:

1. **Being Too Vague**: One of the biggest mistakes is providing too little information. If your prompt lacks detail, the AI might generate something too generic or completely off-target. Avoid prompts like "Design an app screen." Instead, add more specifics like "Design an onboarding screen for a travel booking app with a friendly tone and icons for each step."

2. **Overloading with Information**: On the flip side, providing too much information in a single prompt can overwhelm the AI and lead to confusing or conflicting results. If you try to include too many design elements or instructions in one go, the AI might not be able to prioritize effectively. Break complex prompts into smaller, manageable tasks.

3. **Ignoring Context**: A prompt that lacks context can lead to designs that don't align with the project's purpose or target audience. For example, asking for "a modern UI" without specifying the type of product or the users it's for could result in something too generic. Always provide enough background to guide the AI.

4. **Not Iterating**: Remember that AI-generated designs are not final products—they're starting points. Many designers make the mistake of expecting a perfect result on the first try. Instead, treat the AI's output as a draft that can be refined and improved through additional prompts or feedback.

5. **Neglecting Constraints**: Constraints are your friend when working with AI. They help narrow down the possibilities

and lead to more focused results. Forgetting to specify constraints like color schemes, layouts, or target platforms can lead to designs that don't fit your project's requirements.

* * *

Top AI tools for crafting, refining, and managing effective AI prompts:

1. PromptPerfect - Optimizes prompts to get the best AI results.
2. Jasper - Known for its prompt customization and flexibility.
3. PromptBase - A marketplace to find and share effective AI prompts.
4. Rytr - Provides prompt-building assistance with AI-powered content generation.
5. Copy.ai Templates - Templates to structure and test UX design prompts.
6. PromptLayer - Manages and tracks prompt iterations.
7. Socratic AI - Offers tips and guidance on prompt engineering.
8. PromptHero - For browsing prompt ideas and inspiration.
9. Lexica - A search tool for AI-generated images, useful in prompt refinement.
10. OpenAI Playground - Ideal for hands-on experimentation with prompt structures.

4

Setting Up Your Generative AI Workspace

Now that you understand the fundamentals of Generative AI and the importance of prompt engineering, it's time to dive into the practical side of things: setting up your workspace. Whether you're a solo UX designer or part of a larger team, integrating AI into your design workflow requires the right tools and a structured process. In this chapter, we'll cover the tools you need, how to integrate them seamlessly into your design process, and best practices for collaboration between designers and AI.

Choosing the Right AI Tools for UX Designers

As a UX designer, you have access to an ever-expanding suite of AI tools that can enhance your creative process. However, not all AI tools are created equal, and some are better suited for specific design tasks than others. Below are some of the top Generative AI tools that UX designers should consider incorporating into their workspace:

1. ChatGPT (OpenAI): ChatGPT is an AI language model that excels at generating text-based content. It's a versatile tool for UX designers, particularly when it comes to generating ideas, writing UX copy, or even brainstorming user personas. The conversational nature of ChatGPT makes it a powerful tool for refining your design briefs, testing out user scenarios, or generating content for UI elements like onboarding screens, error messages, and tooltips.

Use Cases:

- Generating user personas based on target demographics
- Writing error messages, button labels, or onboarding instructions
- Ideating new design features by discussing user needs with the AI

Best For: Designers who need help with UX writing, ideation, and generating design specifications.

2. MidJourney: MidJourney is an AI tool designed for generating artistic and creative visuals based on text prompts. It's especially useful for creating mood boards, generating UI mockups, or even brainstorming new design aesthetics. Its creative approach allows designers to explore visual styles that are more abstract or experimental.

Use Cases:

- Creating mood boards or inspiration boards for new design projects

- Generating concept art or visual ideas for user interfaces
- Experimenting with different design aesthetics or color schemes

Best For: Designers looking for inspiration and quick visual mockups.

3. DALL·E (OpenAI): DALL·E is another AI image generator, but it specializes in creating highly specific images from text descriptions. This makes it ideal for UX designers who want to create custom illustrations, icons, or even mockups of user interfaces. DALL·E is particularly helpful for producing quick iterations of design elements, like buttons, banners, or splash screens, without having to spend hours in a graphic design tool.

Use Cases:

- Designing custom icons or illustrations for apps or websites
- Quickly generating UI elements such as buttons, cards, or banners
- Creating conceptual wireframes or mockups to explore new layout ideas

Best For: Designers who need custom visuals and quick iterations of UI components.

4. Figma with AI Plugins: Figma is already a powerhouse in UX design, but by integrating AI plugins, you can make the tool even more powerful. AI-driven plugins like **Magician** for Figma enable designers to create components, wireframes, or even design variants faster. You can use AI to generate color schemes, layout suggestions, or even UI copy directly in Figma, allowing for a more streamlined design process.

Use Cases:

- Generating layout suggestions or UI components in real-time
- Creating quick wireframes or design systems
- Using AI for design critiques or optimization recommendations

Best For: Designers who want AI capabilities integrated directly into their favorite design tool.

5. Adobe Firefly: Adobe Firefly is Adobe's suite of AI-powered creative tools designed for generating images, vector art, and even 3D renders based on text prompts. It's tailored for designers who want high-quality, editable content that can be used in more sophisticated design projects.

Use Cases:

- Creating high-quality, editable vectors for UX design elements
- Generating 3D elements for immersive UX experiences (like AR or VR)
- Exploring different visual styles for design systems

Best For: Designers working on high-fidelity visuals and complex design systems.

* * *

Integrating AI into Your Design Process

The real power of Generative AI comes from its seamless integration into your design workflow. The goal isn't to replace your design process but to enhance it by allowing AI to take over repetitive tasks, generate creative ideas, and speed up iterations. Here's how you can start integrating AI into your everyday design process:

1. Use AI in the Early Stages of Ideation: At the beginning of any UX design project, ideation is key. Instead of staring at a blank canvas, you can use AI tools to generate ideas, mood boards, or even wireframe options. For example, you might use MidJourney or DALL·E to generate a range of visual styles, or ChatGPT to brainstorm potential user flows based on different personas.

Example: You're designing a new app for meal planning. Start by asking ChatGPT for ideas on user flows, like how a user might navigate from adding ingredients to planning a weekly menu. At the same time, you could use MidJourney to generate mood boards featuring different UI styles—whether it's minimalist, colorful, or health-focused.

2. Automate Repetitive Tasks: Once you've established the basics of your design, there are countless tasks that need to be done but don't require heavy creative thinking—like creating button variations, aligning components, or filling in placeholder text. AI tools can automate much of this, saving you time and effort.

Example: Use an AI plugin in Figma to quickly generate button states for hover, clicked, and disabled variations, or to auto-fill lorem ipsum text with AI-generated, context-specific copy.

3. Iteration and Feedback Loops: One of the most time-consuming aspects of UX design is refining and iterating based on feedback. AI can help speed up this process by generating multiple versions of a design element or providing suggestions for improvements.

Example: After conducting a usability test, you might need to adjust a feature based on user feedback. Instead of manually tweaking designs, you can use an AI tool like DALL·E or an AI-powered plugin in Figma to generate new layout options based on the feedback provided.

4. Personalization and A/B Testing: AI can also be incredibly useful for creating personalized user experiences. You can generate multiple versions of the same design for A/B testing or to target different user personas. Generative AI can quickly produce variations in tone, color, and layout, which can then be tested with different user groups.

Example: If you're designing an e-commerce site, you could generate multiple versions of a product page—one targeting younger users with a vibrant, colorful layout and another targeting professionals with a clean, minimalist design. You can then A/B test these versions to see which one performs better.

* * *

Best Practices for Seamless Collaboration Between Designers and AI

The most effective use of Generative AI in UX design happens when there's a strong collaboration between the designer and the AI tool. Here are some best practices to ensure a seamless partnership:

1. Think of AI as a Partner, Not a Replacement: AI isn't here to replace your design expertise. Instead, it's a tool that can help you work faster, iterate more efficiently, and explore creative possibilities you might not have considered. Keep control over the strategic and creative aspects of design, while allowing AI to assist with the more mechanical or repetitive tasks.

2. Iterate Based on AI Outputs: Treat AI-generated designs as starting points, not final products. The first output might not be perfect, but it provides a foundation for you to build on. Always refine and tweak the AI's work to ensure it aligns with the project's goals and user needs.

3. Maintain Human Oversight: AI is a powerful tool, but it lacks the intuition and empathy that human designers bring to the table. Always review AI-generated designs with a critical eye, ensuring they meet accessibility standards, cultural expectations, and user experience goals.

4. Train Your AI with Specific Feedback: Generative AI can improve with guidance. The more specific and detailed your prompts are, the better the AI will understand your needs. Don't hesitate to give feedback after the first output and fine-tune your prompts to get more precise results.

5. Leverage AI for Rapid Prototyping, Not Full Development: AI is incredibly useful for generating ideas and visual assets quickly, but for full-fledged product development, human insight is crucial. Use AI to speed up prototyping, but rely on your expertise and UX testing to finalize the design.

* * *

Top AI tools to establish a UX designer-friendly AI workspace:

1. Figma Plugins (Magician, FigGPT) - AI-enhanced plugins for Figma's design interface.
2. Adobe Firefly - AI-powered creative suite for text-to-image and video edits.
3. Descript - For video and audio editing, helpful in prototyping with voice.
4. Notion AI - Organizes project management and workflow in a design workspace.
5. Google Colab - For running and testing AI code, ideal for tech-savvy UX designers.
6. Zapier - Automates workflows across various tools, enhancing productivity.
7. Slack GPT - Integrates with Slack for seamless AI-driven communication.
8. Miro AI - An AI-powered tool for brainstorming and collaborative design.

9. Claude.ai- Next-generation AI assistant trained to have natural, text-based conversations, and it excels in tasks like summarization, editing, Q&A, decision-making, code-writing, and more.

10. Midjourney Discord Integration - Useful for integrating image generation into discussions.

5

Crafting Prompts for Wireframing and Prototyping

N ow that your Generative AI workspace is set up and you've chosen the right tools, it's time to get into the heart of the design process: wireframing and prototyping. As UX designers, wireframes and prototypes are essential for visualizing ideas, communicating concepts, and iterating on designs. With Generative AI, this process becomes faster and more flexible, enabling you to generate multiple versions of your wireframes and prototypes from a simple prompt.

In this chapter, we'll explore how to craft effective AI prompts for wireframing and prototyping, from low-fidelity sketches to high-fidelity prototypes. You'll also see examples of prompts at different stages of a UX project, so you can easily integrate AI into your workflow no matter the project phase.

How to Generate Wireframes Using AI

At its core, wireframing is about laying out the structural elements of a design. While this is typically a manual process, AI can help speed it up by generating multiple wireframe options based on your requirements. With the right prompts, you can quickly visualize different layouts and decide which one best suits your design goals.

1. Defining the Structure of Your Wireframe: The first step in generating wireframes with AI is to define the basic structure and layout. For example, if you're designing a mobile app, you'll want to specify the key components, such as headers, navigation bars, buttons, and content areas.

Here's an example of how you can use a prompt to generate a basic wireframe layout for a mobile app:

Prompt Example:
"Act as a Wireframe Designer. Create a low-fidelity wireframe for a mobile application that features a top navigation bar, a prominent search bar, a grid layout showcasing product image thumbnails, and a bottom navigation tab with icons for Home, Search, Cart, and Profile. Ensure the wireframe emphasizes user flow and intuitive layout while maintaining clarity in the arrangement of elements."

This simple prompt gives the AI clear instructions on the basic components needed for the wireframe. You can iterate on this by adding more details, such as the type of products being displayed or additional features like filters or sorting options.

2. Adding Interactions and User Flows: Wireframes are not just static layouts; they also need to account for user interactions and flows. By refining your prompt, you can include key interactions and touchpoints within your design.

Prompt Example:

"Act as a Wireframe Designer. Generate a low-fidelity wireframe for a mobile e-commerce application that illustrates the user flow for browsing products, filtering by price, and adding items to the cart. Include the following screens: a product listing page, a product detail page, and a shopping cart screen, ensuring a clear and intuitive user experience throughout."

In this case, the prompt is more detailed, specifying the user flow from browsing to cart addition. This gives the AI enough information to visualize a sequence of wireframes that can later be fleshed out into a full prototype.

* * *

Creating Detailed User Flows and Prototypes with Effective Prompts

As you move from wireframing into prototyping, the level of detail increases. Prototypes simulate real user interactions and can range from simple click-throughs to fully interactive experiences. Crafting the right prompt is essential for ensuring that AI-generated prototypes meet your design goals.

1. Building User Flows with Prompts: User flows map out the journey a user takes through your app or website, from landing on the homepage to completing a task, like signing up for a newsletter or making a purchase. By crafting detailed prompts, you can get AI to generate flow diagrams or even interactive prototypes that show each step.

Prompt Example:

"Act as a User Journey Specialist. Create a user flow diagram for a new user onboarding experience in a fitness application. Outline the journey from account creation through personal details entry, workout preference selection, and setting personalized fitness goals. Each stage should correspond to a clear, interactive screen in the prototype, providing an intuitive and engaging experience that guides the user smoothly through each onboarding step."

With this prompt, you guide the AI to not only generate individual screens but also link them together to show the entire user journey. The result will be a clickable prototype that can be tested for usability.

2. Creating High-Fidelity Prototypes: Once you've tested and refined your low-fidelity wireframes, it's time to move on to high-fidelity prototypes. These are visually polished designs that simulate the final user experience. With AI, you can generate high-fidelity prototypes by adding more specific visual elements to your prompts.

Prompt Example:

"Act as a High-Fidelity Prototype Designer. Create a high-fidelity prototype for a fitness tracking application. The home screen should feature a dashboard displaying weekly progress, a prominent button to start a new workout, and a bottom navigation bar with icons for 'Home,' 'Workouts,' 'Stats,' and 'Profile.' Use a modern, minimalist

design style, incorporating a blue and white color scheme to enhance the user experience."

This level of specificity tells the AI what visual style, color scheme, and elements to include. The AI can then generate a fully fleshed-out high-fidelity prototype based on these details, allowing you to iterate faster and focus on refining the user experience.

* * *

Examples of Prompts for Different UX Project Stages

Let's walk through some example prompts you can use at various stages of a UX project, from initial brainstorming to final prototyping.

1. Low-Fidelity Wireframes (Initial Sketches): These wireframes focus on basic layout and functionality without too much visual detail. AI can help generate simple, structural designs based on the components you need.

Prompt Example:
"Act as a Wireframe Designer. Generate a low-fidelity wireframe for a blog homepage that includes a header, a featured post section, a sidebar for categories, and a list of recent posts. Ensure that the layout is clear and user-friendly, highlighting important content areas for easy navigation."

Prompt Example:

"Act as a Wireframe Designer. Design a wireframe for a mobile application's onboarding screens. Include a welcome screen, user permissions prompts, and tutorial screens featuring simple text and icon placeholders. Ensure that the flow is intuitive and user-friendly, guiding new users through the onboarding process seamlessly."

2. Mid-Fidelity Prototypes (Interactive Flow): In this phase, you're starting to flesh out interactions and flows. AI can help by generating more detailed layouts and linking screens together.

Prompt Example:

"Imagine you are a UI/UX Architect. Design a mid-fidelity prototype for an online banking app. Start with a login screen, then guide the user to an account summary page, followed by a transaction history section, and finally, a form for transferring funds. Map out the entire user journey from login to transfer confirmation, prioritizing clarity, ease of navigation, and a user-friendly flow."

Prompt Example:

"Act as a Prototype Designer. Design a mid-fidelity prototype for an e-learning platform. The flow should encompass a course catalog, a course details page, and a checkout process for enrolling in a course. Ensure that the design is intuitive and user-friendly, facilitating a smooth experience for users as they navigate through the enrollment process."

3. High-Fidelity Prototypes (Final Visuals and Interactions): At this stage, AI-generated designs should be visually polished and include detailed interactions. This is where you can specify style guides, colors, typography, and microinteractions.

Prompt Example:

"Imagine you are designing a high-fidelity prototype for a food delivery app focused on user engagement and ease of access. Start with a home screen that showcases nearby restaurants in a card-style layout, with a prominently placed search bar at the top. Include a bottom navigation bar with icons for 'Home,' 'Orders,' 'Profile,' and 'Favorites.' Aim for a modern, minimal design that incorporates vibrant colors and smooth animations to make interactions enjoyable and intuitive."

Prompt Example:

"Act as a Prototype Designer. Create a high-fidelity prototype for a travel booking website. The landing page should feature a prominently placed search bar allowing users to search for flights, hotels, and car rentals. Include a visually striking hero image in the background that conveys the excitement of travel. Utilize a blue and white color scheme, complemented by modern typography for clear readability and a contemporary look. Ensure that the layout is intuitive, guiding users effortlessly to their desired bookings."

* * *

Common Mistakes to Avoid When Crafting Prompts for Prototyping

While crafting AI prompts for wireframes and prototypes can save you time, there are some common pitfalls to watch out for:

1. Being Too Vague: If your prompt lacks detail, the AI might generate a design that doesn't meet your needs. Always be clear about the key components and flows you want in your design.

34

Example of a Weak Prompt:
  "Generate a wireframe for a mobile app."
  This prompt is too vague and could result in a generic output that doesn't meet your project's requirements.

2. Overloading the Prompt with Too Much Detail: On the flip side, providing too much information can confuse the AI or lead to overly complex designs. Focus on the key elements and flows first, then iterate by adding details.

Example of an Overly Detailed Prompt:
  "Generate a wireframe for a shopping app with a grid of product images, filters for color, size, and brand, a search bar with advanced sorting options, a detailed product description page with multiple sections for reviews, specs, and similar products, and a checkout page with multiple payment options, shipping methods, and promotional codes."

This prompt can overwhelm the AI with too many instructions. Break it down into smaller steps, focusing on one part of the flow at a time.

3. Forgetting to Iterate: AI-generated designs often need fine-tuning. Don't rely on the first output. Instead, use iterative prompts to refine the design and ensure it aligns with your project goals.

* * *

Top AI tools for generating wireframes, prototypes, and layouts:

1. **Motiff** – Generates wireframes based on input text.
2. **Uizard** – Transforms text into wireframes and interactive prototypes.
3. **Whimsical** – Combines AI with wireframing, flowcharts, and UX elements.
4. **Framer AI** – An AI-driven wireframing tool for quick prototyping.
5. **Balsamiq** – Basic wireframing with some AI-assist features.
6. **Sketch2Code** – Converts hand-drawn sketches into digital wireframes.
7. **Marvel** – AI-powered wireframing and prototyping tool.
8. **Mockplus** – Speeds up wireframing with AI-aided design.
9. **Penpot** – Open-source wireframing tool with experimental AI features.
10. **Maze** – Allows for rapid testing of wireframes and prototypes.

6

Visual Design Prompts: From UI Elements to Complete Interfaces

N ow that you've learned how to use Generative AI for wireframing and prototyping, it's time to move into the realm of visual design. This chapter will cover how to craft prompts that can help you generate specific UI components like buttons, icons, and layouts, as well as how AI can assist with color schemes, typography, and branding. You'll also learn how to prompt AI for full-page layouts or entire mobile screens, enabling you to streamline the visual design process and focus more on creativity and refinement.

* * *

Generating Specific UI Components Using AI

At the core of every great user interface are the small components that make it functional and visually appealing—buttons, icons, navigation bars, and more. Instead of spending hours manually designing each element, Generative AI can help you create these components quickly and efficiently by using well-crafted prompts.

1. Designing Buttons with AI: Buttons are one of the most essential UI elements in any digital product. Whether they're used for submitting forms, navigating pages, or confirming actions, buttons must be clear, consistent, and easy to use.

Here's how you can craft a prompt to generate a button design:

Prompt Example:
"Act as a UI Designer. Generate a primary call-to-action button for an e-commerce website. The button should display the text 'Add to Cart' and feature a modern, rounded design. Incorporate a gradient color scheme, ensuring the colors are vibrant yet complementary. Use large, bold text for visibility, and add a subtle drop shadow to create depth and enhance the button's prominence on the page."

This prompt gives the AI specific details about the button's purpose, visual style, and text, which helps it generate an output that aligns with your design vision. You can also tweak the prompt to experiment with different styles, such as flat buttons or minimal designs, depending on your needs.

2. Crafting Icons and Visual Assets: Icons are another crucial part of UI design, providing visual cues and helping users navigate an interface more easily. With the right prompt, you can have AI generate icons that match the visual style of your product.

Prompt Example:

"*Act as a UI Designer. Design a set of minimalist icons for a fitness tracking app. Include icons for 'Workouts,' 'Progress,' 'Settings,' and 'Profile.' Ensure that the icons follow a simple line art style, maintaining a consistent stroke width and spacing throughout the set. The design should be clean and modern, aligning with the overall aesthetic of the app to enhance user navigation.*"

With this prompt, the AI can generate a cohesive set of icons that are visually consistent and aligned with your brand's aesthetic. If you want to explore other styles, you can modify the prompt to request icons in a filled style or with more intricate details.

* * *

AI-Assisted Color Schemes, Typography, and Branding

Beyond generating individual UI components, AI can also assist with creating cohesive visual identities. From choosing harmonious color schemes to selecting typography that matches your brand's tone, AI can simplify the often time-consuming process of building a design system.

1. Generating Color Schemes with AI: Color plays a key role in user experience. The right color scheme can evoke emotions, create visual hierarchy, and reinforce brand identity. AI can help you experiment with color palettes, ensuring they complement each other and align with the overall tone of your design.

Prompt Example:

"Act as a Color Specialist. Develop a color scheme for a financial application designed to inspire trust, professionalism, and a sense of security. Focus on a palette with shades of blue, gray, and white as the primary colors, and include accent colors to add visual interest and guide user attention. Ensure the colors balance well to convey reliability and clarity throughout the user interface."

This prompt gives the AI specific emotional and functional guidance for the color scheme. You can easily tweak the prompt to test different color combinations or find a more playful palette if you're working on a lifestyle or entertainment app.

2. Choosing Typography with AI: Typography helps establish the visual hierarchy of your interface and contributes to the overall brand identity. By giving clear instructions, you can have AI suggest font combinations that are legible, aesthetically pleasing, and consistent with your brand.

Prompt Example:
"Act as a Typography Consultant. Recommend typography for a travel website that conveys a sense of adventure and modernity. Select bold, impactful fonts for headings to create a strong visual presence, while ensuring that body text remains highly legible at smaller sizes. Provide both serif and sans-serif font options to give a balanced, versatile feel across the website."

Here, the AI can provide font pairings that not only look good but also serve the functional requirements of your design. You can further refine the prompt to specify font weights, sizes, or specific font families (e.g., Google Fonts) to better suit your design needs.

3. Branding and Visual Identity: In addition to individual elements like color and typography, AI can assist in generating a complete brand identity that encompasses your visual design choices. By crafting a prompt that outlines your brand's values and aesthetic, you can get AI to generate a visual identity that resonates with your target audience.

Prompt Example:

"Act as a Brand Designer. Develop a visual identity for a wellness brand that embodies calmness, mindfulness, and the beauty of nature. Focus on a palette of soft pastel colors, select clean and serene typography, and integrate minimalist design elements to reflect tranquility and natural harmony throughout the brand's visuals."

This prompt directs the AI to consider the brand's core values and translate them into visual design elements, making it easier for you to create a cohesive brand identity across your UI components, website, and marketing materials.

* * *

Prompting Full-Page Layouts or Mobile Screens

In addition to generating individual UI elements, you can use prompts to create complete page layouts or mobile screens. This allows you to rapidly prototype and iterate on full designs without having to manually arrange each element from scratch.

1. **Full-Page Layouts for Websites:** When designing a full-page layout, it's important to give the AI a clear understanding of the structure and content hierarchy. This includes specifying key components like headers, navigation menus, content sections, and footers.

Prompt Example:
   "Act as a Web Layout Designer. Create a professional and modern homepage layout for a real estate website. Start with a full-width hero image featuring an overlayed search bar, followed by sections for featured properties and client testimonials. Finish with a footer that includes contact information and social media links. Utilize a blue and white color scheme to convey trust and sophistication throughout the design."

This prompt outlines the major components of the homepage, giving the AI enough information to generate a complete, well-structured layout. You can modify the prompt to explore different layouts for other pages, such as property listings, about pages, or contact forms.

2. **Mobile Screen Designs:** Designing for mobile requires careful consideration of screen real estate and user interactions. AI can help you quickly generate mobile screens by using prompts that focus on the flow and layout of the interface.

Prompt Example:
   "Act as a Mobile UI Designer. Craft an engaging onboarding experience for a fitness app that warmly introduces new users. Design a series of screens with a welcoming message, simple prompts to grant location and notification permissions, and a quick tutorial

highlighting key app features. Focus on a minimalist, modern style with vibrant illustrations and clear, bold text to create an approachable, user-friendly start."

In this prompt, the AI focuses on the flow and user interaction, ensuring that the screens are visually consistent and user-friendly. You can extend this prompt to create additional screens, like user profiles, progress tracking, or workout summaries.

* * *

Common Mistakes to Avoid When Crafting Visual Design Prompts

As with wireframing and prototyping, there are common pitfalls to avoid when crafting prompts for visual design.

1. Being Too General: If your prompt is too vague, you might get an overly simplistic design that doesn't meet your expectations. Be specific about the elements and layout you want to see.

Example of a Weak Prompt:
  "Design a landing page for an app."
  This prompt is too general and doesn't provide enough detail for the AI to create a meaningful design.

2. Overloading the Prompt: Overloading your prompt with too many details can overwhelm the AI and result in a cluttered design. Focus on the key elements first, then refine the design in subsequent iterations.

Example of an Overly Detailed Prompt:

"Design a homepage with a hero image, a call-to-action button, a product gallery, testimonials, a blog section, a newsletter signup form, a video embed, and a contact form with social media links."

This prompt is trying to accomplish too much in one go. Break it down into smaller, more manageable sections.

3. Not Iterating on AI-Generated Outputs: AI-generated designs often need refinement. Don't expect the first result to be perfect. Iterate on your prompts and fine-tune the design to ensure it aligns with your goals.

* * *

Top AI tools that assist in creating UI components and full interfaces:

1. **DALL·E** – Generates visuals for UI elements like buttons and icons.
2. **Adobe XD** – With AI plugins for generating UI components.
3. **Canva** – Equipped with AI to suggest layouts, color schemes, and graphics.
4. **Lottie** – For animated icons and assets in interfaces.
5. **Coolors** – Generates color palettes based on input prompts.
6. **UIzard** – Automates UI design for apps and websites.
7. **Magician (Figma plugin)** – Auto-generates images and icons.
8. **Haiku Animator** – Creates interactive, animated UI components.
9. **ColorMind** – AI color palette generator.

10. **Autodraw by Google** – Suggests drawings based on input sketches.

7

Enhancing User Research and Testing with AI

U ser research and testing are critical phases of UX design. They offer insights into how users interact with products, where improvements are needed, and what drives user satisfaction. Traditionally, these processes have been resource-intensive, requiring extensive data analysis, participant recruitment, and multiple iterations. However, Generative AI has opened up new possibilities, helping UX designers streamline these tasks and obtain meaningful insights more efficiently.

In this chapter, we will dive into how AI can assist in analyzing user data, generating survey questions and user testing scenarios, and even automating A/B testing cycles. Through effective prompt engineering, UX designers can improve their ability to conduct research and testing, resulting in more user-centered designs.

Using Prompts for AI to Analyze User Data and Personas

User personas help designers keep the end-user in mind throughout the design process, providing a snapshot of their behaviors, goals, and challenges. Creating personas often requires analyzing large volumes of user data, but AI can speed up this process significantly.

1. Analyzing User Data with AI: Generative AI models can process large datasets, summarizing key insights from user behavior, demographic information, and even feedback from previous iterations of your design. Through specific prompts, you can instruct AI to analyze trends, identify patterns, and segment users into distinct groups.

Prompt Example:
   "Analyze the customer data from our e-commerce website. Break down users by age, gender, browsing behavior, and purchase history to identify three main customer segments."

This prompt directs AI to sift through large datasets and categorize users, helping you target each segment with more precise design decisions.

2. Crafting User Personas: Once AI has analyzed the data, you can use it to craft detailed user personas. These personas should reflect the unique characteristics and needs of different user segments, allowing you to design with greater empathy and focus.

Prompt Example:
   "Act as a UX Researcher. Develop detailed user personas for a fitness app targeting young, frequent mobile users aged 18-24 who

are passionate about fitness. For each persona, include key aspects like motivations, challenges, and specific design needs to enhance their user experience."

With this type of prompt, AI can quickly synthesize data into personas that UX designers can use as a reference for various projects. These AI-generated personas may include motivations, challenges, and potential behavior patterns, helping you tailor the design process accordingly.

* * *

Generating Survey Questions, User Testing Scenarios, and Feedback Loops

Surveys and user testing are essential for gathering direct user feedback on design decisions. AI can assist in generating these tools quickly, allowing for more effective research and testing cycles.

1. Generating Survey Questions: Survey questions need to be clear, unbiased, and relevant to your research goals. AI can generate targeted survey questions based on the specific user experiences you want to measure, helping ensure that the feedback you receive is valuable.

Prompt Example:
"Act as a User Experience Analyst. Devise 10 targeted survey questions aimed at evaluating the checkout process on an e-commerce website. Concentrate on aspects such as user-friendliness, clarity of

instructions, and the overall satisfaction level of customers to gather actionable insights."

This prompt asks AI to craft questions around key user experience metrics, helping you gather actionable feedback on areas that may need improvement.

2. Creating User Testing Scenarios: Effective user testing often involves observing how users perform specific tasks within a design. AI can help you create structured scenarios that guide users through tasks that are critical to the design's success.

Prompt Example:

"Act as a User Experience Researcher. Create three user testing scenarios for a mobile banking app. In the first scenario, a user wants to transfer funds to a friend. Describe how they navigate to the transfer option, input the recipient's details, choose the amount, and confirm the transaction, including any challenges they might encounter, such as entering incorrect information.

In the second scenario, a user needs to check their account balance after making a recent purchase. Illustrate how they locate the account overview and any difficulties they face while trying to find the balance information.

For the third scenario, a user wants to set up a recurring payment for a utility bill. Detail the steps they take to navigate to the payments section, select the biller, enter the payment details, and confirm the setup, noting any potential areas of confusion throughout the process. Ensure each scenario reflects the user's goals and possible pain points."

By generating relevant and realistic user testing scenarios, AI can help you simulate real-world interactions, allowing you to identify issues before a design is fully implemented.

3. Automating Feedback Loops with AI: After gathering feedback through surveys and testing, it's crucial to analyze the results quickly so that you can iterate on the design. AI can speed up this analysis process by extracting insights from user responses and feedback data.

Prompt Example:

"Act as a User Experience Analyst. Analyze feedback gathered from 100 user testing sessions focused on the app's navigation and search functions. Summarize the key findings by identifying the most common pain points users experienced. Highlight issues such as difficulty in locating essential features, confusion with the layout or terminology used in the navigation, and frustrations related to the search functionality, like slow response times or irrelevant search results. Provide insights into how these pain points could impact user satisfaction and suggest potential improvements to enhance the overall navigation and search experience."

AI can process large volumes of feedback far more quickly than manual analysis, helping you focus on the most critical areas for improvement.

* * *

How AI Can Help Streamline A/B Testing and Iteration Cycles

A/B testing allows designers to compare multiple design versions and determine which one performs best with users. AI can automate parts of this process, helping designers generate design variants and analyze test results with greater speed and accuracy.

1. Generating A/B Testing Variants with AI: Creating multiple versions of a design for A/B testing can be time-consuming, especially if you're working with complex layouts. AI can generate variations of a design based on specific guidelines or areas you want to test.

Prompt Example:
"Act as a Website Layout Designer. Create two distinct homepage layout variations for a travel website. The first layout should prominently feature popular destinations with engaging visuals, including a section for top-rated attractions and a user-friendly search bar for travel packages. The second layout should prioritize promotional offers, showcasing special deals and discounts with eye-catching banners, a clear call-to-action for booking, and a dedicated section for limited-time offers. Ensure both designs maintain a cohesive aesthetic and cater to the target audience's travel aspirations."

This prompt allows AI to create two distinct design versions, which you can then present to users to see which one drives better engagement or conversions.

2. Analyzing A/B Test Results with AI: Once an A/B test is complete, AI can assist in analyzing the results, identifying patterns and key metrics such as click-through rates, conversion rates, and user engagement.

Prompt Example:

"Act as a UX Analyst. Review and analyze the results of our A/B test conducted on the homepage design. Examine key metrics related to user engagement, such as time spent on the page, click-through rates, and conversion rates for each design version. Highlight the differences in user behavior and engagement levels, and provide insights on which design performed better based on the data. Finally, recommend the design that should be implemented moving forward, along with potential areas for improvement."

With AI's help, you can gain deeper insights into why one design performed better than another, enabling you to make data-driven decisions on what works best for users.

3. Iterating on Designs Based on AI Insights: After reviewing the results of A/B tests, the next step is to iterate on the design. AI can suggest improvements or additional design variations based on test feedback and performance metrics.

Prompt Example:

"Act as a UX Consultant. Analyze the A/B test results for the homepage layout of our travel website, focusing on user interactions and feedback regarding the booking button's visibility. Suggest specific improvements to enhance the user experience, such as repositioning the booking button for greater prominence, adjusting its size and color for better contrast, and incorporating visual cues or animations to draw attention. Provide detailed recommendations on layout adjustments that can streamline the booking process and facilitate user engagement."

AI can recommend subtle changes, such as improving the

visibility of certain elements or adjusting the layout to enhance the user experience.

* * *

Common Pitfalls to Avoid in AI-Enhanced User Research and Testing

While AI offers significant advantages in streamlining research and testing, there are also some pitfalls you should avoid:

1. Over-Reliance on AI for User Insights: While AI is great at analyzing data, it's important not to overlook the human touch. Always review AI-generated insights critically and supplement them with qualitative research to get a fuller understanding of your users.

2. Failing to Provide Context in Prompts: Be as specific as possible in your prompts. If you ask AI to analyze user data without guiding it toward the most relevant factors, you may receive insights that are too broad or irrelevant to your project.

3. Overcomplicating A/B Testing: A/B testing works best when the variables are clear and simple. Avoid generating overly complex design variations, as they can confuse users and make it difficult to identify which changes lead to improved performance.

* * *

Top AI tools for analyzing user data and enhancing testing processes:

1. **Lookback** – Provides insights by analyzing user testing videos.
2. **A/B Tasty** – AI-powered A/B testing for optimized experiences.
3. **Qualtrics XM** – For data analysis and survey automation.
4. **UserZoom** – For testing and analyzing UX data.
5. **Hotjar** – Heatmaps and behavior tracking.
6. **Synthesia** – Creates AI-driven testing scenarios for diverse personas.
7. **Optimal Workshop** – Offers AI-backed usability testing.
8. **UXCam** – Provides insights by analyzing user interactions.
9. **UsabilityHub** – Assists in user testing with AI-supported data.
10. **Typeform** – AI-generated questions for surveys and user research.

8

Writing Prompts for Accessibility and Inclusion

I n today's digital landscape, ensuring that your designs are both accessible and inclusive is more important than ever. Accessibility ensures that users with disabilities can interact with your product, while inclusivity broadens your design's appeal, catering to users of diverse backgrounds, abilities, and needs. These principles are not just ethical but also necessary for creating user-friendly, legally compliant designs.

Generative AI can play a powerful role in supporting UX designers as they strive to build accessible and inclusive designs. From suggesting accessible design elements to helping you create more inclusive user interfaces, AI can enhance your ability to accommodate all users. In this chapter, we will explore how to write effective prompts that guide AI to suggest accessible and inclusive design solutions.

How to Use AI to Suggest Accessible Design Elements

Accessibility in UX design refers to the practice of making

websites and applications usable by as many people as possible, including those with disabilities. This can include everything from designing keyboard-friendly navigation for users with motor impairments to ensuring that color choices are suitable for users with visual impairments. Generative AI can help UX designers by suggesting accessible design elements and checking the compliance of existing designs with accessibility guidelines.

1. Writing Prompts to Ensure Proper Contrast and Readability: Color contrast is critical in ensuring that text is readable for users with low vision or color blindness. AI can analyze your designs and suggest adjustments to improve contrast and readability.

Prompt Example:

"Act as an Accessibility Specialist. Evaluate the current color scheme of the landing page to identify areas where text contrast falls short of WCAG (Web Content Accessibility Guidelines) standards. Suggest specific changes to enhance text visibility and readability, including adjustments to color hues, saturation, and brightness. Provide alternative color palette options that maintain the page's aesthetic while ensuring that all text elements are easily legible for users with visual impairments."

In response to this prompt, the AI can analyze the contrast between your background and text, suggest more accessible color combinations, and ensure compliance with recognized accessibility standards like WCAG.

2. Generating Accessible Navigation Structures: Keyboard navigation is crucial for users who cannot rely on a mouse. AI can help you design layouts that are easy to navigate using only the keyboard, providing suggestions for tab order, focus states, and more.

Prompt Example:

"Act as a User Experience Designer specializing in accessibility. Develop a fully keyboard-accessible navigation framework for a news website. Detail the ideal tab order to guide users smoothly through the navigation, ensuring that important sections are easily reachable. Describe the design of focus indicators that stand out for users who rely on keyboard navigation. Additionally, provide specific recommendations for implementing ARIA (Accessible Rich Internet Applications) roles for each navigation item to enhance the experience for users with assistive technologies."

This prompt enables AI to create a navigation system that prioritizes accessibility, ensuring that all users, including those with motor impairments, can easily navigate your site.

3. Suggestions for Alternative Text for Visuals: Alternative text (alt text) is essential for users who rely on screen readers. Well-written alt text ensures that images and other non-text content are accessible to visually impaired users.

Prompt Example:

"Act as an Accessibility Specialist. Create detailed alt text descriptions for the images featured on this e-commerce product page. Ensure the alt text conveys not only the content of the images but also their purpose and context within the shopping experience. Focus on providing clarity for users relying on screen readers, highlighting

key features of the products, such as colors, sizes, and any unique attributes that would assist users in making informed purchasing decisions."

This prompt can help AI generate meaningful alt text that goes beyond merely describing the image, instead focusing on the image's purpose and how it contributes to the user's overall experience.

* * *

Prompts for Generating Inclusive UX Designs that Cater to Diverse Users

Inclusive design means considering the full range of human diversity, including factors like race, gender, age, and culture. With the help of AI, you can create designs that cater to a broader spectrum of users, ensuring that no one feels excluded from the experience.

1. Creating Culturally Sensitive Design Elements: Designs that cater to global audiences must account for cultural nuances and sensitivities. AI can assist by generating design elements that avoid cultural bias and are relevant across different regions and cultures.

Prompt Example:
   "Act as a Cultural Design Consultant. Create a culturally inclusive design layout for a global e-learning platform. Ensure that the imagery used reflects diverse cultures and backgrounds, avoiding stereotypes. The language should be clear and respectful, using

neutral terminology that appeals to a wide audience. Additionally, recommend a color scheme that is harmonious and culturally sensitive, avoiding colors that may have negative connotations in specific cultures. Provide suggestions for layout features that enhance accessibility and foster an inclusive learning environment for users from different cultural contexts."

This prompt instructs the AI to create a design that takes cultural differences into account, ensuring that the platform feels welcoming and appropriate for users from different regions.

2. Designing for Different Age Groups: Different age groups interact with technology in unique ways. AI can help generate designs that are age-appropriate and easy to use for various demographics, from children to older adults.

Prompt Example:
"Act as an Age-Inclusive UI Designer. Create a user interface for a health and wellness app tailored for users aged 18 to 65. Ensure that the design accommodates the varying needs of different age groups by implementing adjustable text sizes for readability and using clear, intuitive navigation that caters to all ages. Include interaction methods that are accessible to users with varying levels of tech-savviness, such as larger touch targets for older users and swipe gestures for younger users. Additionally, suggest features that enhance usability for each age group, ensuring a seamless experience across the entire age spectrum."

By using this prompt, AI can create designs that cater to a wide age range, ensuring that features like readability and interaction methods are user-friendly for everyone, regardless of age.

3. Generating Gender-Neutral and Inclusive Designs: Inclusivity also extends to gender-neutral language and imagery. AI can help generate designs that avoid stereotypes and ensure that all users, regardless of gender identity, feel comfortable interacting with the product.

Prompt Example:

"Act as an Inclusive Design Specialist. Create a gender-neutral registration form for a fitness app. Ensure the form uses inclusive language that welcomes all users, regardless of their gender identity. Include options that go beyond binary selections, such as 'Non-binary,' 'Genderqueer,' and an open field for users to specify their identity if they wish. Additionally, design the form to minimize assumptions about the user's identity while maintaining a straightforward layout that enhances usability for everyone."

AI can help you create more inclusive forms and user flows that accommodate non-binary and gender-fluid users, ensuring a more welcoming and supportive environment for all users.

* * *

Using AI to Check and Improve the Accessibility of Existing Designs

AI is also capable of analyzing your existing designs and identifying areas where accessibility and inclusivity could be improved. This process is not just about fixing issues but also about proactively enhancing the user experience for all users.

1. Conducting an Accessibility Audit with AI: Before launching a product, it's essential to audit your design for accessibility compliance. AI can help identify issues like improper color contrast, missing alt text, or non-keyboard-friendly navigation.

Prompt Example:

"Act as an Accessibility Auditor. Conduct a thorough accessibility audit of this website based on WCAG standards. Identify specific areas for improvement, focusing on aspects such as color contrast to ensure text is easily readable against background colors, the adequacy of alt text for images to enhance understanding for users relying on screen readers, and the effectiveness of keyboard navigation to ensure all interactive elements can be accessed without a mouse. Provide detailed recommendations for each identified issue to enhance overall accessibility."

In response to this prompt, AI can quickly scan your design and highlight areas where it falls short of accessibility standards, giving you a clear roadmap for improvement.

2. Improving Existing Designs for Visual Impairments: Even if your design is functional, it may not fully accommodate users with visual impairments. AI can suggest enhancements to improve the overall experience for visually impaired users, such as offering better magnification options or suggesting alternative color schemes.

Prompt Example:

"Act as an Accessibility Consultant. Review the interface of this app and identify specific improvements tailored for users with visual impairments. Suggest enhancements such as incorporating adjustable text size options for better readability, implementing high-contrast mode settings to facilitate visibility, and providing

alternative color schemes that maintain usability. Additionally, recommend the inclusion of screen reader compatibility features to ensure a seamless experience for all users."

By using this prompt, AI can identify areas where your design could be optimized for visually impaired users, ensuring they can navigate and interact with your product more easily.

3. Testing for Screen Reader Compatibility: Screen readers are used by visually impaired users to interpret on-screen content. Ensuring that your design is compatible with screen readers is crucial for accessibility. AI can help test for compatibility and suggest improvements to enhance the experience for screen reader users.

Prompt Example:

"Act as a Usability Tester. Evaluate the compatibility of this e-commerce website with screen readers. Conduct a thorough assessment of the site's navigation, product descriptions, and checkout process. Provide detailed feedback on areas where the screen reader experience may be lacking, such as missing alt text for images, unclear headings, or inadequate labeling of form fields. Suggest specific improvements to enhance accessibility and ensure a smooth user experience for individuals relying on assistive technology."

AI can simulate screen reader interactions and flag issues like missing ARIA labels, untagged images, or unclear navigation paths, helping you fine-tune your design for better accessibility.

* * *

Common Pitfalls to Avoid When Using AI for Accessibility and Inclusion

While AI is a powerful tool for enhancing accessibility and inclusivity, it's important to avoid certain pitfalls:

1. Overlooking the Human Element: AI can suggest accessible elements, but it's still vital to involve real users, particularly those with disabilities, in the design and testing process. Relying solely on AI-generated insights may lead to oversights that real users could catch.

2. Applying a One-Size-Fits-All Approach: Accessibility and inclusivity are not about applying generic solutions. Ensure your prompts are specific to the needs of your users, whether you're designing for mobility impairments, cognitive disabilities, or diverse cultural backgrounds.

3. Ignoring Context-Specific Needs: Different contexts require different approaches to accessibility and inclusion. For example, a high-contrast design might work well for a user with low vision but could cause strain for other users. Always tailor your AI-generated solutions to the specific use case.

* * *

Top AI tools for ensuring inclusive, accessible designs:

1. **Stark** – Checks accessibility for contrast, color blindness, etc.
2. **A11Y Color Palette** – Generates accessible color combina-

tions.

3. **Wave (Web Accessibility Evaluation Tool)** – Reviews designs for accessibility.

4. **Equal Entry's Accessibility Checker** – For accessible UX guidance.

5. **axe DevTools** – Analyzes and suggests accessible improvements.

6. **Accessibility Insights** – Helps to create inclusive interfaces.

7. **Ally.js** – JavaScript library for accessible interface components.

8. **Color Oracle** – Simulates color blindness for inclusive design.

9. **AccessiBe** – AI tool that helps improve accessibility compliance.

10. **Be My Eyes** – Uses AI and human volunteers to test accessibility.

9

Creating AI-Enhanced Design Systems

D esign systems are the backbone of consistent and scalable user experiences. They provide a cohesive set of guidelines, components, and visual standards that help designers and developers work together efficiently and deliver unified interfaces across products. With Generative AI, UX designers can create robust, prompt-based design systems that streamline workflows, maintain brand consistency, and allow for flexibility and innovation.

In this chapter, we'll explore how AI can support UX designers in building adaptable design systems and component libraries, maintaining a consistent design language, and creating patterns that meet the needs of both users and stakeholders. We'll also look at best practices to ensure that working with AI doesn't compromise the flexibility or creativity of your designs.

How to Develop Prompt-Based Design Systems and Libraries

Design systems are composed of reusable components, visual assets, and guidelines that form the building blocks of a product.

With AI-driven prompt engineering, designers can quickly generate new elements, iterate on design components, and create a library that adapts to different product needs. Prompt-based design systems allow UX designers to maintain consistency while still accommodating the unique requirements of individual projects.

1. Crafting Core Components with AI Prompts: From buttons and icons to typography and color schemes, Generative AI can assist in the rapid creation of core components. By defining prompts that outline each component's purpose, style, and function, designers can generate multiple variations and refine them to fit the design system.

Prompt Example:
"Act as a UI Element Designer. Create a primary call-to-action button for an e-commerce app. The button should feature a rounded shape that aligns with the brand's blue and white color scheme. Incorporate a subtle shadow to give it a modern, three-dimensional effect. Ensure the button includes the text 'Shop Now' in bold, legible typography, and provide options for hover and active states to enhance user interaction."

This type of prompt allows AI to create a button that aligns with your design system's aesthetic, while still allowing for easy adjustments or variations as needed.

2. Building a Component Library with Flexibility: A component library is most effective when it can adapt to various design needs without losing consistency. AI can help by generating variations on basic components, giving designers a starting point for customization based on specific project requirements.

Prompt Example:

"Act as a UI/UX Designer. Generate three distinct variations of the navigation bar for a SaaS platform, ensuring each version caters to different user needs and screen sizes.

1. ***Compact Version:*** *Design a streamlined navigation bar suitable for mobile devices, focusing on essential features. Include a hamburger menu icon for easy access, and ensure the design is intuitive, with icons representing key functions like Dashboard, Notifications, and Profile.*
2. ***Standard Version:*** *Create a standard navigation bar for tablet and small desktop views. This version should display a horizontal layout with clearly labeled menu items such as Home, Features, Pricing, and Support. Incorporate dropdown menus for subcategories, ensuring a balance between aesthetics and functionality.*
3. ***Expanded Version:*** *Develop an expanded navigation bar for larger desktop displays. This design should showcase all menu items prominently, including additional sections like Resources and Blog. Utilize hover effects for dropdowns and consider adding a search bar integrated into the navigation for improved accessibility. Ensure that the design aligns with the overall branding of the SaaS platform, with a focus on user-friendly navigation and a modern aesthetic."*

By prompting AI to produce different versions of a component, designers can maintain a unified look across products while allowing for adaptability in different contexts and screen sizes.

3. Generating Style Guides and Usage Documentation: Effective design systems include documentation that guides team members on component usage and styling. AI can assist in creating these guides, making it easier for developers and designers to follow best practices and maintain consistency across the product.

Prompt Example:

"Act as a UI Documentation Specialist. Generate comprehensive documentation for our brand's primary button component. Include best practices for sizing, color options, and different states such as hover, active, and disabled. Emphasize the importance of accessibility and consistency in implementation to maintain brand integrity."

Through prompts like this, AI can quickly generate comprehensive usage guides that help team members implement components in a way that maintains the integrity of the design system.

* * *

Consistent Design Languages with the Help of AI-Generated Patterns

A consistent design language is essential for building a cohesive user experience, especially in products with multiple pages, features, or applications. AI can help by generating consistent design patterns, such as layout grids, color schemes, and typography choices, that align with your brand's style and improve usability.

1. Establishing a Unified Color and Typography Palette: Colors and fonts are key elements of any design language. AI can help establish a consistent color palette and font hierarchy that reflect your brand identity while enhancing readability and visual appeal.

Prompt Example:

"Act as a Color Strategy Expert. Design a cohesive color palette for a health app aimed at promoting user well-being and trust. Choose blue as the foundational color, and identify additional accent colors that support a calming atmosphere. Explain how each color contributes to the app's user experience and its alignment with the values of health and wellness."

By defining tone and purpose, this prompt directs AI to develop a color palette that reinforces the brand's message and maintains visual coherence across components.

2. Defining Layout Grids and Spacing Rules: AI can also assist in creating layout grids and spacing rules, which are essential for ensuring that designs are visually balanced and easy to navigate. With well-defined prompts, you can quickly generate layout guides for both desktop and mobile platforms.

Prompt Example:

"Act as a Layout Designer. Create a 12-column grid structure for a news website layout. Provide detailed guidelines on spacing and padding to ensure consistent white space throughout the design. Include recommendations for how to effectively use the grid to enhance readability and visual hierarchy in the content."

This prompt allows AI to create layout structures that are visually cohesive and adaptable, ensuring that elements are aligned and spaced evenly for a polished final product.

3. Developing Iconography and Illustrative Styles: Consistent iconography and illustrations contribute to a unified visual language. With Generative AI, you can quickly develop a library of icons and images that align with your brand and are easy to update as needed.

Prompt Example:
"Act as an Icon Designer. Create a set of minimal, line-style icons for a financial app. The icons should represent key functionalities, including 'Account,' 'Transaction,' 'Settings,' and 'Notifications.' Ensure the design maintains a consistent stroke width and style to fit seamlessly within the app's overall aesthetic."

This prompt allows AI to create icons that fit seamlessly within your design system, ensuring visual consistency across the app.

* * *

Best Practices for Maintaining Flexibility While Working with AI

One of the main advantages of a well-structured design system is that it provides flexibility, enabling designers to modify components and layouts without losing consistency. When integrating AI into your design system, it's essential to balance the efficiency AI provides with the creative freedom that UX designers need.

1. Starting with Clear Guidelines for AI-Generated Content: To keep AI-generated components consistent with your design system, start with clear guidelines for elements like colors, fonts, and component dimensions. Establishing these rules helps AI create assets that align with your system's standards.

Prompt Example:
"Act as a UI Component Designer. Generate a sidebar menu for a dashboard that adheres to the following design guidelines: use blue as the primary color, apply Open Sans for the font, set the icon size to 24px, and ensure there is an 8px spacing between each item. This will ensure consistency with the overall design system."

By defining specific standards, this prompt ensures that the AI's output will be compatible with your existing components, saving you time on adjustments.

2. Encouraging Designer Review and Iteration: While AI can create a range of components and layouts quickly, it's essential that designers still review and refine these assets. AI should serve as a tool to speed up the design process, not as a replacement for the human touch that adds creativity and empathy to user experiences.

Prompt Example for Review:
"Act as a UI Designer. Generate three variations of a call-to-action banner for an educational website, focusing on clarity and usability. Ensure that these designs are aligned with the brand's identity and maintain consistency in user experience. Designers should review each variation for alignment with brand guidelines and overall effectiveness."

71

This approach keeps designers engaged in the process, ensuring that the final product is refined and user-centered.

3. Regularly Updating and Evolving the Design System: A design system is a living document that should evolve as your brand and user needs grow. AI can be invaluable in keeping your design system up to date by quickly generating new components or styles based on updated brand guidelines.

Prompt Example:
   "Update the button styles in the component library to reflect the new brand color palette and add a soft shadow to enhance accessibility."

By utilizing AI to refresh components based on current brand standards, you can maintain a design system that is both consistent and adaptable.

* * *

Common Pitfalls to Avoid When Creating AI-Enhanced Design Systems

Incorporating AI into your design system offers great advantages, but there are some potential challenges to keep in mind:

1. Losing Human-Centric Design:
   AI can generate functional components, but it lacks the understanding of user emotions and behaviors that human designers bring. Always review AI-generated elements to ensure they enhance the user experience.

2. Over-Complicating Prompts for Routine Elements:

Simple components like buttons or icons don't need overly complex prompts. Stick to clear, concise prompts that provide essential guidelines and save more intricate prompts for complex elements.

3. Becoming Over-Reliant on AI for Creativity

While AI is a fantastic productivity tool, it can't fully replicate human creativity. Use AI to speed up routine tasks but always leave room for innovation and experimentation by human designers.

* * *

Tools for building and managing design systems:

1. **Figma Libraries** – Organize and maintain design components.
2. **Zeroheight** – Document and manage design systems collaboratively.
3. **Storybook** – For creating and testing design components.
4. **Material Design** – Google's UI/UX design system framework.
5. **InVision DSM** – Manages scalable design systems.
6. **Polaris** – Shopify's design system tool.
7. **Supernova** – Manages and automates design systems.
8. **Interplay** – Supports design-to-code in design systems.
9. **Deco IDE** – AI-enhanced design system editor.
10. **Handoff** – Simplifies component sharing with developers.

10

Collaborative Design: AI + Human Teams

I n today's fast-paced design environment, collaboration between UX designers, developers, and stakeholders is essential for building user-centered products. Generative AI can play a transformative role in bridging gaps between teams, improving communication, and streamlining documentation, making the entire process more efficient and aligned.

This chapter delves into how UX designers can use prompt engineering to enhance collaboration with developers, facilitate clear communication within teams, and create alignment among stakeholders. By exploring real-world examples and best practices, you'll gain insights into harnessing AI as a unifying force in your design projects, enabling you to produce cohesive and effective designs more efficiently.

How UX Designers Can Use Prompts to Collaborate Better with Developers

The relationship between designers and developers is critical to turning creative concepts into functional products. However, differences in workflows, terminology, and priorities can sometimes lead to miscommunication. AI-generated prompts can help streamline this collaboration by creating clear, concise handoff materials and bridging the knowledge gap between design and development.

1. Using Prompts to Generate Component Specification

Generative AI can assist UX designers in producing detailed component specifications, making it easier for developers to understand and implement designs. By specifying dimensions, colors, states, and behaviors through prompts, designers can ensure that the final product matches their vision.

Prompt Example:

"Act as a Component Specification Generator for a UX design project. Generate comprehensive specifications for a login button that includes the following details:

- **Size:** *120 pixels wide by 40 pixels high.*
- **Color:** *Use the primary brand color (hex code: #3498db) for the button background.*
- **Font:** *Apply Roboto Bold at 14 pixels for the text, with white (#ffffff) for the button label.*
- **Text Alignment:** *Center the text both vertically and horizontally within the button.*
- **Hover State:** *Define the hover state as a darker shade of the primary color (hex code: #2980b9) to indicate interactivity.*
- **Disabled State:** *Specify a disabled state with a gray background (#bdc3c7) and gray text (#7f8c8d) to indicate unavailability.*
- **Border Radius:** *Set the border radius to 5 pixels for a rounded*

appearance.
- **Action:** *The button should navigate to the login page upon clicking.*
- **Accessibility:** *Include ARIA labels for screen readers to enhance accessibility (e.g., aria-label="Login button").*

Ensure that the specifications are clear, concise, and structured in a way that developers can easily understand and implement the design accurately."

Through prompts like these, AI can output specifications that reduce ambiguity, helping developers implement designs accurately without requiring additional clarification from designers.

2. Creating Responsive Layouts and Breakpoints

Responsive design is essential for UX, but the specifics of adaptive layouts can sometimes be challenging for developers to interpret. AI-generated prompts can help designers outline layout adaptations for various screen sizes, providing developers with a roadmap for implementing responsive designs.

Prompt Example:
"Act as a Layout Specification Generator for a UX design project. Generate detailed layout specifications for a three-column blog page, ensuring that it is responsive across different devices. For the desktop view, the layout should feature three equal columns, each taking up 30% of the width, with a 5% margin between them. The overall page width should be set at 1000 pixels and centered, with 20 pixels of padding around the main content area to enhance readability.

When adapting for tablet devices, set a breakpoint at 768 pixels to switch to a two-column layout. Each column should be 48% wide, with a reduced 4% margin between them, and padding around the main content should be adjusted to 15 pixels for a better fit.

For mobile views, set a breakpoint at 480 pixels where the layout should transition to a single-column format, taking up 100% width. The padding should be further reduced to 10 pixels to optimize space.

Additionally, include specifications for a sticky header that spans the full width of the page and a footer with a height of 60 pixels to ensure it remains at the bottom. The background color of the page should be a light gray (#f9f9f9) to create contrast with the text content. Ensure that the specifications are clear and organized for easy implementation by developers."

By using prompts to define these specifications, designers ensure that developers have clear, actionable instructions for creating layouts that adapt smoothly across devices.

3. Automating Design Handoffs and Documentation

Generative AI can help generate and organize documentation for design handoffs, including guidelines on using components, color schemes, and typography. This AI-generated documentation allows both designers and developers to stay on the same page without repetitive explanations or follow-up questions.

Prompt Example:

"Act as a Design Handoff Document Generator for an e-commerce application. Generate a document that outlines the primary components of the app, including buttons, input fields, and product cards. Include spacing guidelines to ensure consistent margins and padding across all screens. Specify color usage for backgrounds, text, and accents, ensuring they align with the brand's palette. Lastly, describe the navigation flow, highlighting key user paths from the

home page to product checkout. The document should be concise yet comprehensive enough for developers to implement the design accurately."

This prompt allows AI to produce a structured document that developers can refer to, minimizing potential miscommunications and speeding up the handoff process.

* * *

AI-Assisted Team Communication and Documentation

Effective communication within design teams is essential to ensure that everyone remains aligned on project goals, milestones, and deliverables. AI can enhance internal communication by generating clear, concise summaries of design updates, creating documentation for feedback loops, and even facilitating stand-up meeting notes.

1. Summarizing Design Changes for Team Updates

Keeping teams updated on design iterations can be time-consuming. With Generative AI, designers can prompt summaries of significant updates, making it easier for team members to stay informed on the project's progress and understand design decisions without needing extensive meetings.

Prompt Example:

"Summarize the design changes made to the onboarding flow, including new color schemes, updated icons, and adjustments to user input fields based on recent feedback."

78

By creating automated summaries, AI helps streamline team updates, allowing designers and other stakeholders to focus on their respective tasks.

2. Documenting Feedback Loops and Iterations

Generative AI can track feedback and iteration cycles by generating prompts to document and summarize key points from user testing sessions, stakeholder feedback, or peer reviews. This documentation provides a transparent record of decisions and adjustments, making it easier for teams to reference past discussions when needed.

Prompt Example:

"Generate a summary of feedback from the recent stakeholder review on the mobile app design. Include key points on user flow improvements, color adjustments, and text readability."

This approach ensures that valuable feedback is captured and accessible to all team members, improving accountability and helping maintain a user-centered design focus.

3. Using AI to Generate Meeting Agendas and Follow-Ups

AI can also assist in organizing meetings by creating clear agendas and post-meeting follow-ups. With prompt-based agendas, teams can cover essential topics without veering off track, and AI-generated follow-ups ensure that everyone is clear on their action items.

Prompt Example:

"Create a meeting agenda for the design-development sync, including discussion points on the onboarding flow, responsive

layouts, and accessibility updates."

After the meeting, AI can summarize action items, allowing teams to refer back to the follow-up without needing to sift through extensive notes.

* * *

Examples of Using AI to Align Stakeholders and Design Teams

Stakeholders play a key role in the success of UX projects, but they may not always understand the technicalities of the design process. AI can help bridge this gap by generating simplified explanations of complex design concepts, creating visual representations, and aligning stakeholders with the design team's goals and methodologies.

1. Translating Technical Design Concepts for Stakeholders

When presenting to stakeholders, it's important to communicate design decisions in a way that is accessible to non-designers. Generative AI can help by generating layman-friendly explanations and visual examples, making it easier for stakeholders to understand and approve designs.

Prompt Example:
"Explain the concept of responsive design for a stakeholder who is unfamiliar with UX terminology. Use simple language and provide examples of a website adapting to different screen sizes."

This approach helps stakeholders grasp essential design concepts, fostering alignment and reducing the likelihood of mis-communication during reviews and approvals.

2. Creating Visual Roadmaps and Timelines

Visual roadmaps and timelines can help stakeholders understand project progress and milestones. With prompt-based AI, designers can quickly generate visual assets that illustrate the project journey, allowing stakeholders to see the bigger picture and anticipate upcoming phases.

Prompt Example:

"Generate a visual project timeline for the mobile app redesign, highlighting key phases: research, wireframing, prototyping, user testing, and final launch."

Providing stakeholders with an overview of the project roadmap helps build trust and provides context for the design team's pace and objectives.

3. Generating Prompt-Based User Scenarios for Stakeholder Review

AI can assist in creating realistic user scenarios and flows that illustrate how the end product will function. These user scenarios help stakeholders visualize the user journey and better understand how specific design elements contribute to the overall experience.

Prompt Example:

"Create a user scenario for a first-time user signing up for our fitness app. Include steps from account creation to browsing workout options."

Scenarios like these make it easier for stakeholders to empathize with users, ensuring that everyone is aligned on design decisions that improve usability and engagement.

* * *

Best Practices for Leveraging AI in Collaborative Design

Working with AI in collaborative design settings requires a balanced approach. Here are some best practices to ensure that your team makes the most of AI's potential:

1. Encourage Regular Designer-Developer Collaboration
AI can help with prompt-based documentation and specifications, but face-to-face (or virtual) meetings between designers and developers are still invaluable. Encourage open communication to clarify any AI-generated instructions and address specific project needs.

2. Use AI to Support, Not Replace, Human Insights
AI can generate summaries, scenarios, and specifications, but it cannot replicate human intuition, creativity, and empathy. Always review AI-generated content and use it as a supplement to human understanding.

3. Customize Prompts Based on Audience
When creating prompts for stakeholders, team members, or developers, adjust the prompt's complexity and focus to match the audience. For stakeholders, keep language simple and focused on high-level concepts; for team members, include

technical specifics.

* * *

Tools that facilitate team collaboration in AI-enhanced environments:

1. **Slack with GPT Integration** – AI-powered communication and collaboration.
2. **Miro AI** – Brainstorming and collaborative design sessions.
3. **Zoom with AI Transcription** – AI-supported calls and design discussions.
4. **Figma Multiplayer** – Real-time collaboration on design files.
5. **Jira** – AI for task management and collaboration.
6. **Dropbox Paper** – Collaborative workspace with AI for design documentation.
7. **Basecamp** – Project management and team communication.
8. **Asana** – AI-assisted project management.
9. **Confluence** – Knowledge-sharing tool with AI suggestions.
10. **Airtable** – AI-enhanced database for collaborative projects.

11

Ethical Considerations in AI-Powered UX Design

As AI becomes increasingly integral to UX design, ethical considerations are essential. From addressing biases in AI-generated outputs to maintaining a human-centered approach, the ethical landscape is complex but vital for responsible AI-powered design. The decisions made during the design process directly affect user experience, inclusivity, and, ultimately, society. This chapter explores how UX designers can engage with AI responsibly, ensuring that AI supports a diverse and equitable experience for all users. We'll delve into how to recognize and mitigate bias, preserve human-centered design principles, and prepare for the ethical challenges that lie ahead as AI continues to evolve.

Addressing Bias in AI-Generated Designs

AI models are only as objective as the data they're trained on, and data often reflects historical biases present in our society. These biases can manifest in AI-generated designs, which may unwittingly exclude certain groups or reinforce stereotypes.

For UX designers, understanding and addressing bias in AI-generated outputs is critical to building inclusive products.

1. Recognizing and Understanding Bias in AI Outputs

Bias in AI often results from patterns in training data, which may include demographic, cultural, or socioeconomic imbalances. For example, an AI model trained predominantly on Western design preferences might fail to capture the nuances of cultural contexts in other regions, leading to designs that feel irrelevant or even alienating to diverse audiences.

Prompt Example:

"Create a color scheme and layout for a multilingual, multicultural app interface that celebrates diversity. The design should incorporate elements that resonate with various cultural backgrounds while avoiding stereotypes. Highlight the significance of each design choice in fostering inclusivity and representation."

Using prompts that explicitly request diverse perspectives can help mitigate bias by encouraging the AI to consider a broader range of design elements, accommodating a variety of user groups.

2. Techniques to Minimize Bias in AI-Generated Designs

When using AI tools, UX designers can minimize bias by actively auditing and adjusting AI outputs to ensure they are fair and inclusive. Considerations include testing designs with diverse user groups and continually refining prompts to promote inclusivity.

Prompt Example:

"Evaluate the AI-generated design for cultural sensitivity, en-suring it represents a balanced perspective that honors diverse global design styles rather than favoring Western aesthetics. Provide feedback on areas for improvement and suggest alternatives that enhance inclusivity."

By prioritizing inclusive designs through intentional prompt engineering, UX designers can make AI more sensitive to cultural differences, helping prevent the perpetuation of stereotypes.

3. Building Diverse and Representative Training Data

Though UX designers may not control the data directly, feedback to AI providers and developers can play a role in improving the AI's fairness. By advocating for diverse, representative datasets and testing models on varied use cases, designers help encourage a more ethical approach to data collection and training.

* * *

Ensuring Human-Centered Design with AI

AI may enhance efficiency, but it is essential to keep the user at the heart of every design decision. Human-centered design emphasizes empathy, understanding, and responsiveness to real user needs. As UX designers leverage AI, they must ensure that technology serves these principles, maintaining an authentic connection with users.

1. Balancing Automation with Empathy

While AI can handle repetitive design tasks, it lacks the innate empathy that human designers bring. To uphold human-centered design principles, UX designers should use AI to complement—rather than replace—their intuitive, human insights.

Prompt Example:

"Create a user-friendly interface for a healthcare app that prioritizes empathy and accessibility for older adults with limited technology experience. The design should feature large, readable text, straightforward navigation, and supportive prompts that guide users through tasks while considering their emotional and physical needs."

Prompts like this remind the AI to consider emotional aspects that resonate with users, ensuring that design outputs align with user-centric goals.

2. Using AI to Enhance User Empathy

AI can actually help designers develop a deeper understanding of their users by generating personas and empathy maps that provide insights into user needs. This, in turn, can lead to more human-centered designs.

Prompt Example:

"Develop an empathy map for a user persona who faces frequent accessibility challenges online. Include key pain points, goals, and emotional responses, as well as suggestions for design improvements that can better support their needs."

By encouraging the AI to highlight user emotions and experiences, designers gain insights into how to make digital spaces more compassionate and accessible.

3. Regular Testing and Feedback Loops with Real Users

It's essential for AI-generated designs to undergo real-world testing with users. Testing ensures that designs meet actual user needs, preserving human-centeredness in the face of increasingly automated design tools.

Prompt Example:

"Generate a survey for user feedback on the accessibility of the AI-generated interface, including questions on usability, comfort, and emotional response."

Designers can integrate user feedback into future AI iterations, maintaining alignment with the core principles of human-centered design.

* * *

Future Ethical Challenges in AI and UX

The rapid evolution of AI brings challenges that will shape the future of UX and ethical design. Issues like data privacy, deepfake technology, and the potential for AI to fully automate certain design tasks raise concerns about the role and impact of AI in society. Preparing for these challenges allows UX designers to adapt and respond responsibly.

1. Data Privacy in AI-Driven Design

As AI becomes more embedded in UX workflows, user data

88

will likely play an even larger role in creating tailored experiences. Maintaining data privacy in AI-driven design is vital to protecting user information and ensuring trust.

Prompt Example:
"Generate data collection guidelines for an AI-driven app that balance personalization with strict user privacy protections."

Prompts like this can help guide the AI in generating designs that prioritize user privacy, encouraging transparent data practices that meet ethical standards.

2. Navigating Intellectual Property and AI-Created Content

The question of ownership in AI-generated designs is complex. If AI generates unique assets for a design, who owns the rights to those assets? UX designers must be aware of evolving intellectual property laws and ensure that their AI-generated work respects the creative contributions of others.

Prompt Example:
"Generate unique design assets for a website using only original AI outputs and document the process to ensure IP compliance."

By staying informed on legal developments and taking proactive steps to verify compliance, UX designers can safeguard their designs and avoid potential copyright issues.

3. Anticipating the Social Implications of AI in UX

As AI-generated designs become more widespread, UX professionals must consider the broader societal impacts, from job displacement to changes in how people interact with digital products. Preparing for these shifts allows designers to take an ethical, proactive approach.

Prompt Example:
 "Generate a brief report on the societal implications of AI-driven design, with a focus on user autonomy, job roles in UX, and long-term effects on user interaction."

By prompting AI to assess its own implications, UX designers can gain valuable insights into the future trajectory of AI and its potential impact on the workforce, user experience, and society.

* * *

Tools and platforms for ethical AI use and bias reduction:

1. **AI Fairness 360 (IBM)** – For identifying and mitigating AI bias.
2. **Pymetrics** – AI with fairness checks for inclusivity.
3. **Google's What-If Tool** – Testing model bias and fairness.
4. **EthicsKit** – Ethical AI guidelines and practices.
5. **DataRobot** – Automated machine learning with bias evaluation.
6. **FairML** – Tool for fairness-aware AI model assessment.
7. **Harkness.ai** – Ethical monitoring tool.
8. **ExplainX AI** – For model transparency and accountability.
9. **Clarifai** – Bias detection in visual content.
10. **AI Explainability 360** – Evaluates transparency in AI systems.

12

Advanced Prompt Engineering: Pushing Boundaries

With a strong foundation in the basics of prompt engineering, UX designers can begin to explore more advanced techniques, pushing the limits of what Generative AI can offer. Advanced prompt engineering enables designers to craft sophisticated, multi-layered prompts that guide AI in producing more complex, nuanced, and innovative design concepts. In this chapter, we'll look at ways to create intricate designs through complex prompts, experiment with AI-driven creativity, and tackle unique design challenges such as immersive experiences in augmented and virtual reality (AR/VR).

Crafting Complex, Multi-Layered Prompts for Sophisticated Designs

While basic prompts can generate simple UI elements and layouts, complex designs often require a deeper level of detail. Multi-layered prompts enable AI to process a variety of factors in tandem—such as user journey, brand identity, and accessibility requirements—producing designs that feel cohesive and purposeful.

1. Structuring Multi-Layered Prompts

To build a sophisticated prompt, consider each component of the design independently, then merge them into a single, comprehensive prompt. This approach enables you to guide AI step-by-step through complex requirements, creating outputs that align closely with your vision.

Prompt Example:

"Act as a UI/UX Designer. Generate a modern, high-fidelity mobile screen layout for a fintech app, emphasizing a minimalist style that ensures strong contrast for optimal readability. Incorporate essential components, including a user profile header, a transaction history section, and an interactive budgeting chart. Use a color palette that resonates with a young professional brand image, while also ensuring accessibility by implementing features like large tap targets and high color contrast for users with varying visual abilities."

With such a prompt, AI can provide a detailed layout that integrates style, function, and accessibility. Each layer of the prompt contributes to the final design, creating a nuanced output that's ready for refinement.

2. Combining User Journeys with Visual Design

Designing around user journeys requires that AI understand the flow of interaction as well as the aesthetics. Multi-layered prompts can incorporate user flows alongside visual specifications, guiding AI to produce designs that both look good and serve specific functions within the user journey.

Prompt Example:

"Generate a desktop UI for an online learning platform's course module page. Include a progress tracker at the top, a sidebar for course contents, and a main area for video playback. Emphasize visual cues that keep the user oriented, such as breadcrumbs and highlighted text sections. Keep the colors calm and neutral to avoid visual fatigue."

This approach aligns the layout and visuals with user needs, ensuring that each design element serves the intended flow and user journey.

3. Iterative Refinement Through Prompt Variations

Sometimes, generating a sophisticated design requires trying out several variations of the same prompt. By iterating on prompts, designers can compare results and refine aspects that require adjustment, making prompt engineering a dynamic, explorative process.

Prompt Example:

"Generate three variations of a product page layout for an e-commerce platform. Prioritize clean and modern design, large product images, a prominent "Add to Cart" button, and user review sections. In each variation, adjust layout styles for product recommendations, ratings, and filtering options."

This iterative approach allows designers to assess multiple perspectives on the same concept, guiding AI to explore different interpretations that can inspire further refinement.

* * *

Experimenting with AI to Create Innovative Design Concepts

Generative AI offers opportunities to experiment with novel design ideas that might be difficult to envision manually. By crafting prompts that encourage creativity, designers can explore groundbreaking concepts, blending styles, layouts, and elements in ways that go beyond traditional design approaches.

1. Encouraging AI to Break Conventions

Traditional design rules are valuable, but AI allows designers to push beyond these constraints by requesting out-of-the-box ideas. This experimental approach often leads to fresh, unexpected solutions that can redefine a brand's aesthetic.

Prompt Example:

"Generate an unconventional homepage layout for a travel app aimed at Gen Z, emphasizing an abstract, collage-style aesthetic with playful animations, bold typography, and vibrant colors. Include a dynamic navigation menu that shifts as users scroll."

By encouraging AI to "break the rules," designers can uncover innovative layouts and aesthetics that create memorable experiences and stand out in a crowded market.

2. Using AI for Style Fusion and Cross-Disciplinary Inspiration

Advanced prompt engineering allows designers to combine diverse styles, such as minimalism with a retro color palette, or futuristic layouts with natural textures. AI can facilitate these "style fusion" concepts, drawing inspiration from different artistic disciplines to generate unique and engaging designs.

Prompt Example:

"Create a futuristic but organic-themed UI for a meditation app. Use soft, earth-tone gradients combined with clean, geometric shapes and subtly animated transitions. The design should feel both high-tech and serene, like a digital oasis."

Prompts that combine seemingly contrasting styles inspire AI to craft designs that resonate on multiple levels, creating a hybrid aesthetic that can set brands apart.

3. Prompting for Unconventional Layouts and Interactions

Generative AI also enables designers to explore new types of layouts and interactions that diverge from standard UX practices. Designers can prompt AI to create interfaces with unconventional flows, like circular navigation or animated scroll effects, helping create experiences that are immersive and surprising.

Prompt Example:
"Generate a portfolio website layout for an artist, with a radial navigation menu and parallax scrolling effects. Emphasize interactivity by including motion effects as users explore each section. The overall style should feel like a virtual art gallery."

By guiding AI to explore unique layouts, designers can create experiences that draw users in and challenge their expectations, resulting in memorable and interactive designs.

* * *

Leveraging AI for Unique Design Challenges (e.g., Immersive Experiences, AR/VR)

Designing for emerging fields like augmented and virtual reality requires a different approach than traditional UX. Generative AI can support these unique challenges by assisting in the visualization of immersive interfaces, three-dimensional components, and spatial interactions.

1. Prompting for AR/VR UI Elements

Designing for AR and VR requires prompts that account for spatial relationships, user movements, and realistic depth. AI can help create interfaces that adapt to the user's physical space, maintaining functionality while enhancing immersion.

Prompt Example:

"Generate an augmented reality UI for an interactive museum exhibit. Include icons that float at arm's reach, translucent overlays for information, and interactive hotspots that reveal details when users gaze at them. Emphasize an elegant, museum-quality aesthetic."

With such prompts, designers can prototype immersive interfaces that guide users smoothly through a 3D space, providing an engaging experience that feels natural and intuitive.

2. Crafting Prompts for Spatial and Interactive AR Elements

In AR environments, UI elements need to interact with real-world objects and respect user movement. AI can generate interfaces that adapt to these considerations, ensuring that visual elements integrate seamlessly with physical surroundings.

Prompt Example:

"Act as an AR Interface Designer. Create a wayfinding interface for an augmented reality shopping mall map. The design should feature

floating arrows that update in real-time as the user navigates, an interactive floor directory, and personalized store recommendations based on the user's current location. Prioritize visibility and ease of understanding to enhance the user experience while ensuring intuitive navigation throughout the mall."

By prompting AI to visualize these spatial interfaces, designers can build intuitive experiences that blend digital information with physical spaces, aiding users in navigation and interaction.

3. Designing for Emotional Engagement in Virtual Environments

The immersion of VR offers an opportunity to evoke emotions through design. AI can help create visual and interactive elements that contribute to the overall mood and experience, whether it's the calm of a meditation app or the excitement of a virtual event.

Prompt Example:

"Generate a calming virtual environment for a VR wellness app. Include soft ambient lighting, gentle animations of leaves and water, and minimal, natural-sounding UI interactions. The design should evoke a peaceful forest setting."

By prompting AI to generate emotionally resonant visuals and interactions, designers can create VR experiences that go beyond functionality, deeply engaging users on an emotional level.

13

Integrating Generative AI as a Catalyst for UX Innovation

A s we close this guide, it's clear that Generative AI stands poised to revolutionize the field of UX design. By combining the power of prompt engineering with a deep understanding of user experience, designers can unlock entirely new ways of creating, iterating, and refining digital experiences. This final chapter synthesizes the key takeaways and provides actionable steps for integrating Generative AI into your design workflows to remain competitive, relevant, and creatively fulfilled in a rapidly evolving digital landscape.

1. Embracing Generative AI as a Tool, Not a Replacement

A central theme throughout this book has been positioning AI as a collaborative partner rather than a replacement for human creativity. The capabilities of AI to analyze patterns, generate designs, and streamline workflows are extraordinary, but they thrive best when guided by a designer's vision and intuition. Human empathy, ethical judgment, and cultural awareness remain irreplaceable components in creating designs that resonate on a deeper level with users. AI empowers designers to amplify their strengths, focus on strategic aspects of design, and approach UX from a new, innovative perspective.

* * *

2. *Key Takeaways: How to Leverage AI for UX Success*

To summarize, here are the essential steps and principles for effectively integrating AI into your design processes:

- **Master Prompt Engineering**: Crafting effective prompts is an art in itself. With clear, structured, and intentional prompts, you can influence AI outputs to align with your design objectives, ensuring consistency with your brand's vision and user needs.
- **Select the Right Tools**: Different AI tools excel at different aspects of UX. By choosing the right mix—whether it's ChatGPT for ideation, DALL·E for visual assets, or Midjourney for layout exploration—you can create a productive AI-enhanced workspace.
- **Experiment and Iterate**: Successful AI integration involves a mindset of experimentation. Test various prompt structures, explore unorthodox design suggestions, and use rapid prototyping to iterate quickly. AI enables designers to go beyond conventional ideas, fostering a culture of innovation.
- **Collaborate Cross-Functionally**: AI can act as a bridge between design, development, and product teams. By generating clear and detailed documentation, user flows, and even code snippets, AI helps streamline collaboration

across the entire product team.
- **Prioritize Ethical and Inclusive Design**: With great power comes great responsibility. As designers, it's crucial to use AI in ways that promote inclusivity, mitigate bias, and ensure accessibility. Be vigilant about the ethical implications of AI in UX and prioritize human-centered values in every project.

* * *

3. Practical Steps for Implementation

For those ready to bring Generative AI into their organizations, consider the following practical steps:

- **Start Small**: Begin with low-stakes projects, such as creating simple UI elements, wireframes, or branding assets, to get comfortable with the AI's capabilities.
- **Train Your Team**: Upskill your design team in prompt engineering and familiarize them with AI's potential applications in UX. Training can significantly enhance productivity and ensure that designers approach AI from a strategic angle.
- **Integrate AI Early in the Design Process**: Incorporate AI during the ideation and wireframing stages to benefit from rapid iterations and insights. Using AI early allows for faster testing and evolution of design concepts, which can be refined further by the team.
- **Define Metrics for Success**: Measure the impact of AI on your design workflows and user experience outcomes. Track efficiency improvements, user engagement metrics, and

overall design quality to assess how well AI integration is working for your team.

* * *

4. Envisioning the Future of AI-Enhanced UX Design

The journey of incorporating Generative AI into UX design is just beginning. With each advancement, from more nuanced prompt understanding to greater personalization capabilities, AI is set to become a cornerstone of digital experience creation. This book has aimed to prepare you for that future, equipping you with the foundational skills and strategies to leverage AI effectively, ethically, and creatively.

As Generative AI tools evolve, UX designers will find even more ways to blend human-centered insights with machine-driven efficiency. This convergence offers an unprecedented opportunity to shape user experiences that are not only more engaging but also profoundly attuned to user needs and behaviors. By staying informed, adaptable, and open to AI's potential, UX designers can lead the way in crafting digital worlds that inspire, connect, and resonate deeply with users.

In the end, the promise of AI in UX design is about expanding what's possible. It's about empowering designers to dream bigger, create faster, and design more inclusively. By embracing Generative AI thoughtfully and strategically, you're not only enhancing your own skills but also paving the way for a new era in design—one where human empathy and machine intelligence work hand in hand to create experiences that are both innovative and meaningful.

www.ingramcontent.com/pod-product-compliance
Lightning Source LLC
Chambersburg PA
CBHW071300050326

40690CB00011B/2472